Look and See

Susannah Reed

NATIONAL
GEOGRAPHIC
LEARNING

Australia • Brazil • Mexico • Singapore • United Kingdom • United States

Scope and Sequence

		Words	Structure	Value	Letters and Sounds/ Numbers	Content Connections	
						Video	Project
1 Hello! p. 5		Hello! Goodbye. Say hello. Wave goodbye. Stand up. Sit down. Open your book. Close your book.	How are you? I'm fine, thank you.	Make friends.	Aa /æ/	**Social Science** How do people say hello around the world?	A puppet
2 School p. 11		school apron bag chair crayon pencil table	What's this? It's a pencil.	Take care of your things.	1, 2	**Social Science** How are classrooms different around the world?	A pencil holder
3 Colors p. 17		paint blue green orange purple red yellow	What color is the book? It's red.	Be creative.	Ee /ɛ/	**Art** What happens when we mix primary colors?	A squish painting
4 Toys p. 23		train ball bus car doll puppet teddy bear	I have a ball.	Share your toys.	3, 4	**Social Science** What land transportation do we use?	A bus collage
5 Let's Move! p. 29		body arms feet hands head legs tummy	Touch your head. Move your hands.	Be active.	Ii /ɪ/	**Music, Physical Education** What are different ways to dance?	A shaker

Look and See 1

		Words	Structure	Value	Letters and Sounds/ Numbers	Content Connections	
						Video	Project
6 **Food** p. 35		apple banana carrot cracker milk orange water	I like oranges. Me, too!	Choose healthy food.	5, 6	**Science** How do plants grow?	An apple tree book
7 **My Family** p. 41		photo brother dad grandma grandpa mom sister	This is my mom.	Be good to your family.	Oo /a/	**Science** Do animals live in families?	A photo frame
8 **On the Farm** p. 47		chicken cat cow dog goat horse sheep	Is it a cow? No, it isn't. Is it a horse? Yes, it is.	Take care of animals.	7, 8	**Science** What do we get from farm animals?	A paper-plate sheep
9 **My Clothes** p. 53		hat jacket shoes shorts socks T-shirt black, brown, white	My T-shirt is orange. My shorts are red.	Dress yourself.	Uu /ʌ/	**Social Science** How is wool made into clothes?	A yarn sweater
10 **Outside** p. 59		frog bird fish flower leaf rainbow tree	How many birds? Four birds.	Explore outside.	9, 10	**Science** What animals use camouflage?	A camouflaged animal picture

Girls shaking hands at school, Bangladesh

What's your name?

My name's Jian.

STRUCTURE: *What's your name? My name's Jian.*

1 Look and see. **2** TR: 0.1 Listen and say. **3** TR: 0.2 Listen and sing. **4** TR: 0.3 Sing and do.

Hello!

Happy children at
school, Mongolia

LESSON 1

NEW WORDS: *Hello!, Goodbye.*

1 Look and see. **2** SC: 1 Watch. **3** TR: 1.1 Listen and say. **4** TR: 1.2 Listen and do.

5

Open your book.

Close your book.

Stand up.

Sit down.

Wave goodbye.

Say hello.

LESSON 2

NEW WORDS: *Say hello. Wave goodbye. Stand up. Sit down. Open your book. Close your book.*

1 TR: 1.3 Listen and point.   **2** TR: 1.4 Listen and do.   **3** TR: 1.5 Listen again and do.

How are you?

I'm fine, thank you.

STRUCTURE: *How are you? I'm fine, thank you.*

1 TR: 1.6 Listen and point. **2** TR: 1.7 Listen and say. **3** Play and say.

Friends playing together,
Malaysia

VALUE

Make friends.

LESSON
4

SONG AND VALUE: *Make friends.*

1 TR: 1.8 Listen and point.　**2** TR: 1.9 Listen and sing.　**3** TR: 1.10 Sing and do.　**4** Stick.

alligator

A ↓ .... **a**

Aa ↓ ....

LESSON 5

LETTERS AND SOUNDS: Aa, /æ/

1 TR: 1.11 Listen and point. **2** TR: 1.12 Listen. Trace and say. **3** TR: 1.13 Listen and chant. **4** Draw and say.

9

**Inupiaq children saying
hello, Alaska, USA**

LESSON
6

VIDEO   Content Word: *world*
1 Look and see.   **2** SC: 2 Watch.   **3** SC: 2 Watch and say.

LESSON
7

PROJECT
1 Make.

School

A girl on her way to school,
Ivory Coast

LESSON 1

NEW WORD: *school*

1 Look and see.   **2** SC: 3 Watch.   **3** TR: 2.1 Listen and say.   **4** TR: 2.2 Listen and do.

11

apron

bag

pencil

table

crayon

chair

Boy at school,
Guatemala

LESSON 2

NEW WORDS: *apron, bag, chair, crayon, pencil, table*

1 TR: 2.3 Listen and point. **2** TR: 2.4 Listen and say. **3** TR: 2.5 Listen and chant.

12

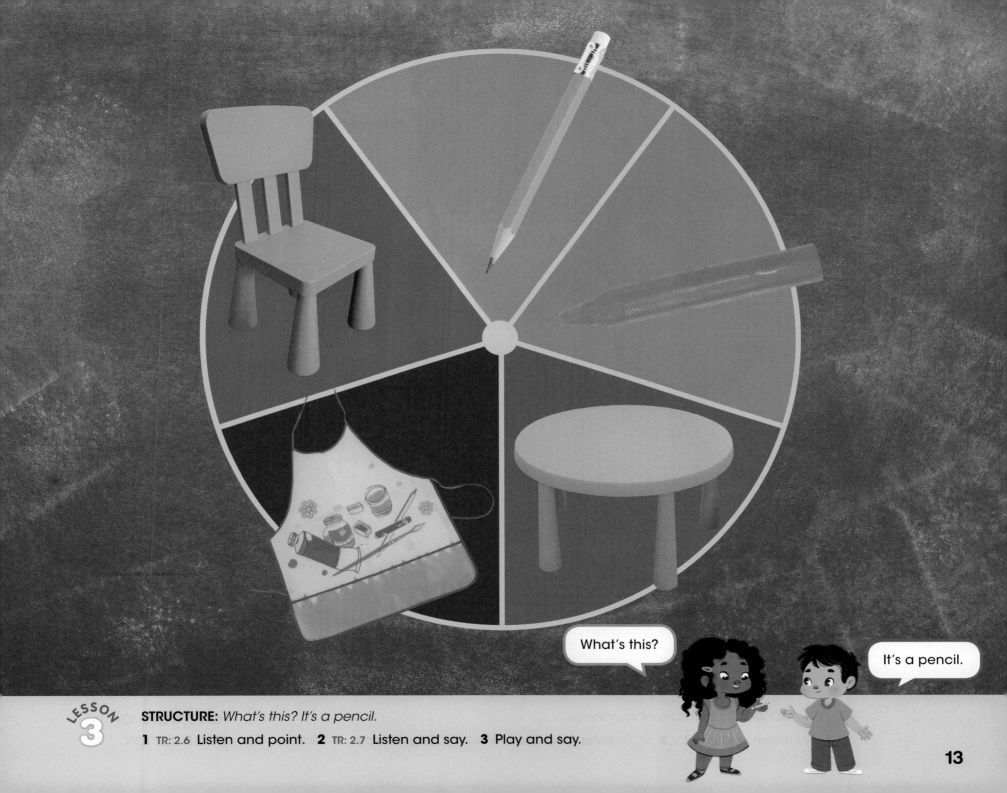

STRUCTURE: *What's this? It's a pencil.*

1 TR: 2.6 Listen and point.   **2** TR: 2.7 Listen and say.   **3** Play and say.

LESSON 3

13

Boys reading together, UAE

LESSON 4

SONG AND VALUE: *Take care of your things.*

1 TR: 2.8 Listen and point.   **2** TR: 2.9 Listen and sing.   **3** TR: 2.10 Sing and do.   **4** Stick.

14

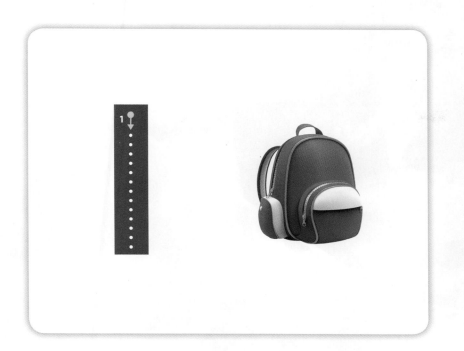

LESSON 5

NUMBERS: 1, 2

1 TR: 2.11 Listen and point.   **2** TR: 2.12 Listen. Trace and say.   **3** TR: 2.13 Listen and chant.   **4** Draw and count.

15

LESSON 6   VIDEO   Content Words: *classroom, different, fun, teacher*
1 Look and see.   2 SC: 4 Watch.   3 SC: 4 Watch and say.

LESSON 7   PROJECT
1 Make.

Colors

A girl covered in paint

NEW WORD: *paint*

1 Look and see. **2** SC: 5 Watch. **3** TR: 3.1 Listen and say. **4** TR: 3.2 Listen and do.

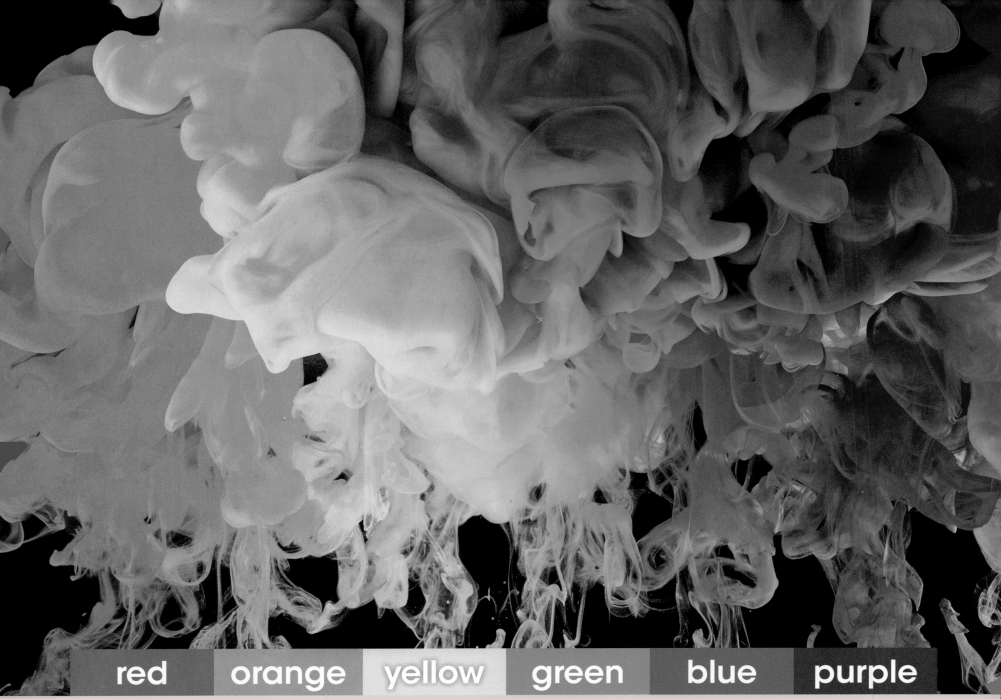

red	orange	yellow	green	blue	purple

LESSON
2

NEW WORDS: *blue, green, orange, purple, red, yellow*

1 TR: 3.3 Listen and point. **2** TR: 3.4 Listen and say. **3** TR: 3.5 Listen and chant.

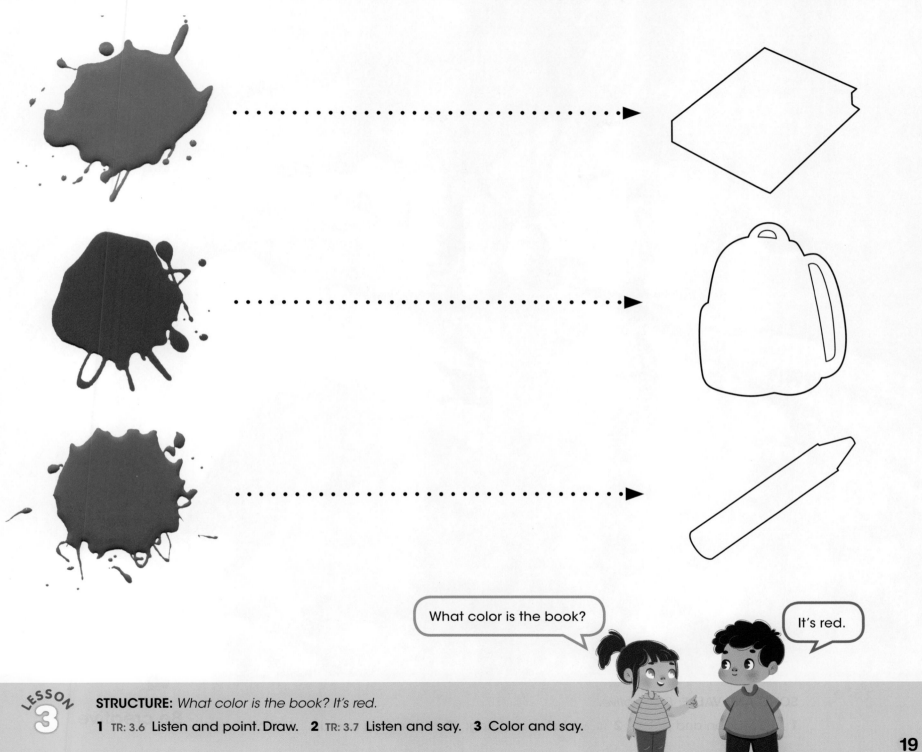

What color is the book?

It's red.

LESSON
3

STRUCTURE: *What color is the book? It's red.*

1 TR: 3.6 **Listen and point. Draw.**   **2** TR: 3.7 **Listen and say.**   **3 Color and say.**

19

A child with artwork,
Brazil

VALUE

Be creative.

SONG AND VALUE: *Be creative.*

1 TR: 3.8 Listen and point. **2** TR: 3.9 Listen and sing. **3** TR: 3.10 Sing and do. **4** Stick.

elephant

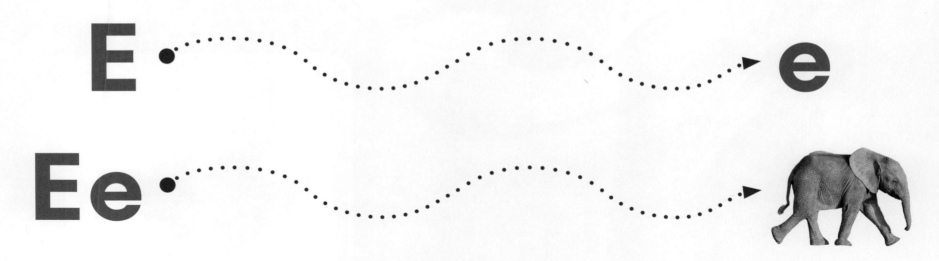

E • e

Ee •

LESSON 5

LETTERS AND SOUNDS: Ee, /ɛ/

1 TR: 3.11 Listen and point.   **2** TR: 3.12 Listen. Trace and say.   **3** TR: 3.13 Listen and chant.   **4** Draw and say.

21

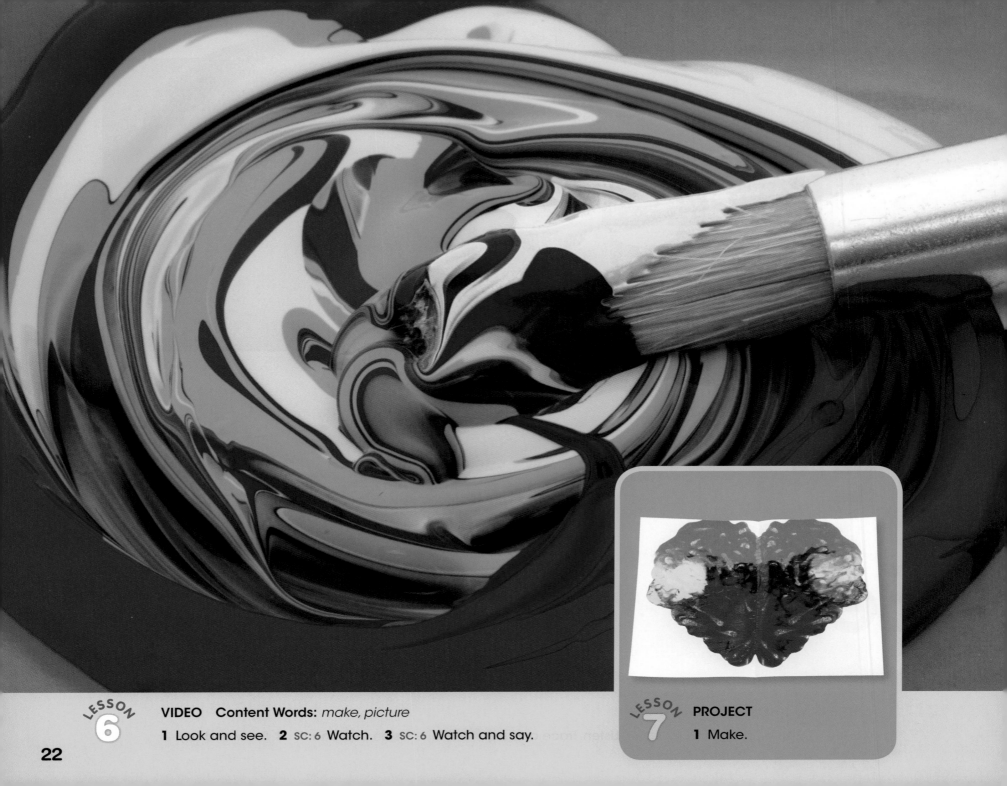

VIDEO   **Content Words:** *make, picture*

LESSON **6**

1 Look and see.   **2** SC: 6 Watch.   **3** SC: 6 Watch and say.

22

LESSON **7**

PROJECT

1 Make.

Toys

A train show at the New York Botanical Garden, USA

LESSON 1

NEW WORD: *train*

1 Look and see. **2** SC: 7 Watch. **3** TR: 4.1 Listen and say. **4** TR: 4.2 Listen and do.

23

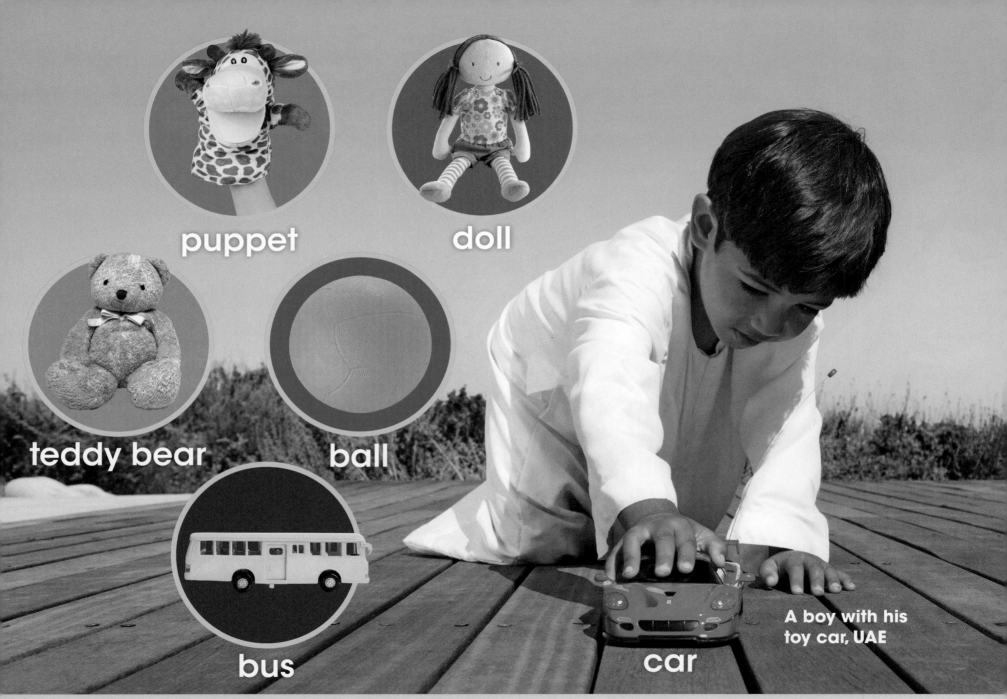

puppet

doll

teddy bear

ball

bus

car

A boy with his toy car, UAE

LESSON 2

NEW WORDS: *ball, bus, car, doll, puppet, teddy bear*

1 TR: 4.3 Listen and point.   **2** TR: 4.4 Listen and say.   **3** TR: 4.5 Listen and chant.

24

I have a ball.

Two.

LESSON 3

STRUCTURE: *I have a ball.*

1 TR: 4.6 Listen and point. **2** TR: 4.7 Listen and say. **3** Play and say.

25

LESSON 4

SONG AND VALUE: *Share your toys.*

1 TR: 4.8 Listen and point. **2** TR: 4.9 Listen and sing. **3** TR: 4.10 Sing and do. **4** Stick.

VALUE

Share your toys.

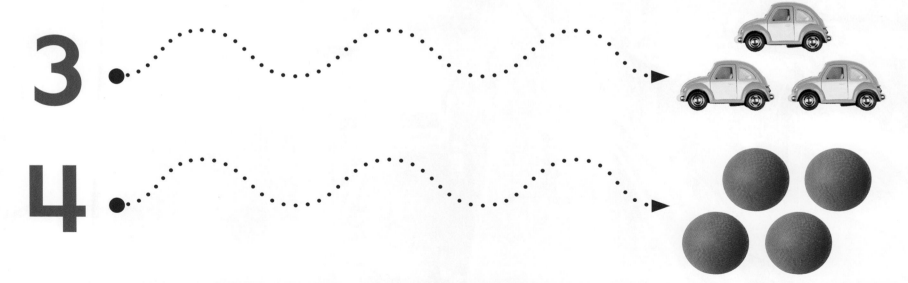

LESSON
5

NUMBERS: 3, 4

1 TR: 4.11 Listen and point. **2** TR: 4.12 Listen. Trace and say. **3** TR: 4.13 Listen and chant. **4** Draw and count.

27

Trains, buses, and cars, Malaysia

LESSON 6

VIDEO Content Words: *big, pink, small*

1 Look and see. **2** SC: 8 Watch. **3** SC: 8 Watch, point, and say.

LESSON 7

PROJECT

1 Make.

Let's Move!

A boy practicing
kung fu, China

LESSON
1

NEW WORD: *body*

1 Look and see. **2** SC: 9 Watch. **3** TR: 5.1 Listen and say. **4** TR: 5.2 Listen and do.

29

hands

head

arms

legs

tummy

feet

LESSON
2

NEW WORDS: *arms, feet, hands, head, legs, tummy*

1 TR: 5.3 **Listen and point.** **2** TR: 5.4 **Listen and say.** **3** TR: 5.5 **Listen and chant.**

30

touch

move

Touch your head.

Move your hands.

Children dancing together,
China

VALUE

Be active.

LESSON
4

SONG AND VALUE: *Be active.*

1 Look and see. **2** TR: 5.8 Listen and do. **3** TR: 5.9 Listen and sing. **4** Stick.

32

iguana

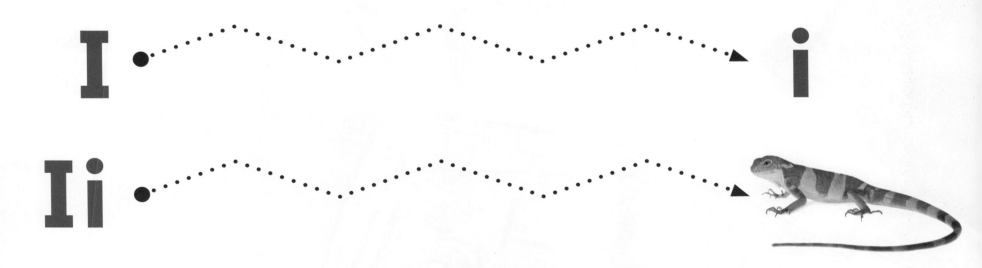

LETTERS AND SOUNDS: Ii, /ɪ/

1 TR: 5.10 Listen and point.　**2** TR: 5.11 Listen. Trace and say.　**3** TR: 5.12 Listen and chant.　**4** Draw and say.

Dancers at a festival, Mexico

VIDEO Content Words: *clap, dance, left, right, stomp*
1 Look and see. **2** SC: 10 Watch. **3** SC: 10 Watch and do.

LESSON
7
PROJECT
1 Make.

34

Food

An apple orchard, USA

LESSON 1

NEW WORD: *apple*

1 Look and see.   **2** SC: 11 Watch.   **3** TR: 6.1 Listen and say.   **4** TR: 6.2 Listen and do.

35

carrot

cracker

banana

orange

milk

water

LESSON 2

NEW WORDS: *banana, carrot, cracker, milk, orange, water*

1 TR: 6.3 **Listen and point.**   **2** TR: 6.4 **Listen and say.**   **3** TR: 6.5 **Listen and chant.**

 I like oranges.

 Me, too!

LESSON 3

STRUCTURE: *I like oranges. Me, too!*

1 TR: 6.6 Listen and point. **2** TR: 6.7 Listen and say. **3** Color and say.

37

A fruit market, Indonesia

SONG AND VALUE: *Choose healthy food.*

1 TR: 6.8 Listen and point.   **2** TR: 6.9 Listen and sing.   **3** TR: 6.10 Sing and do.   **4** Stick.

VALUE

Choose healthy food.

 LESSON 5

NUMBERS: 5, 6

1 TR: 6.11 Listen and point. **2** TR: 6.12 Listen. Trace and say. **3** TR: 6.13 Listen and chant. **4** Draw and count.

39

VIDEO   Content Words: *grow, plant, seed, tree*
1 Look and see.   **2** SC: 12 Watch.   **3** SC: 12 Watch, point, and say.

PROJECT
1 Make.

My Family

A family celebration, China

LESSON 1

NEW WORD: *photo*

1 Look and see.   **2** SC: 13 Watch.   **3** TR: 7.1 Listen and say.   **4** TR: 7.2 Listen and do.

41

A family, India

mom

dad

grandpa

sister

brother

grandma

sister

me

NEW WORDS: *brother, dad, grandma, grandpa, mom, sister*

1 TR: 7.3 **Listen and point.** **2** TR: 7.4 **Listen and say.** **3** TR: 7.5 **Listen and chant.**

STRUCTURE: *This is my mom.*

1 TR: 7.6 Listen and point.   **2** TR: 7.7 Listen and say.   **3** Draw and say.

A boy and his grandma, Slovakia

VALUE

Be good to your family.

SONG AND VALUE: *Be good to your family.*

1 TR: 7.8 Listen and point.   **2** TR: 7.9 Listen and sing.   **3** TR: 7.10 Sing and do.   **4** Stick.

44

octopus

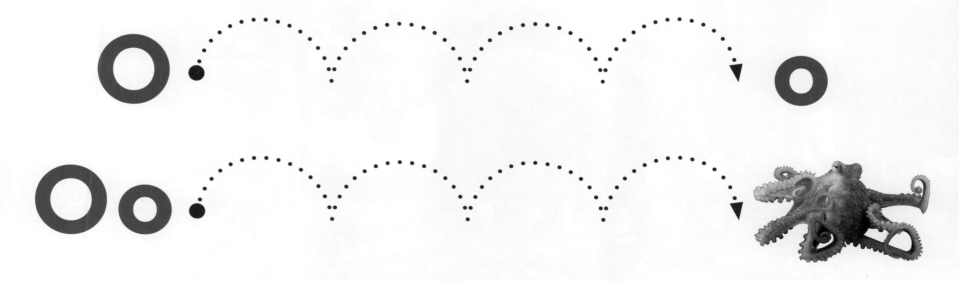

LETTERS AND SOUNDS: Oo, /ɑ/

1 TR: 7.11 Listen and point.   **2** TR: 7.12 Listen. Trace and say.   **3** TR: 7.13 Listen and chant.   **4** Draw and say.

45

Lions and elephants, Kenya

LESSON 6

VIDEO Content Words: *baby, cub, lion*

1 Look and see. **2** SC: 14 Watch. **3** SC: 14 Watch, point, and say.

LESSON 7

PROJECT

1 Make.

On the Farm

Chickens leaving their coop, USA

 LESSON 1

NEW WORD: *chicken*

1 Look and see. **2** SC: 15 Watch. **3** TR: 8.1 Listen and say. **4** TR: 8.2 Listen and do.

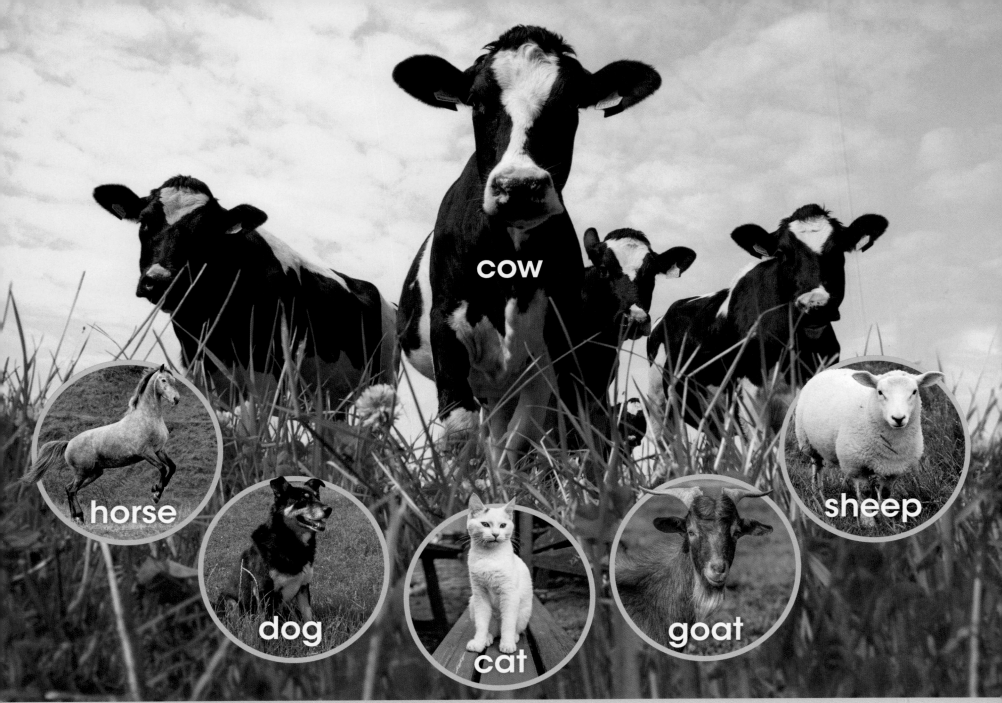

cow

horse

dog

cat

goat

sheep

LESSON 2

NEW WORDS: *cat, cow, dog, goat, horse, sheep*

1 TR: 8.3 Listen and point.   **2** TR: 8.4 Listen and say.   **3** TR: 8.5 Listen and chant.

48

Is it a cow?

No, it isn't.

Is it a horse?

Yes, it is.

STRUCTURE: *Is it a cow? No, it isn't. Is it a horse? Yes, it is.*

1 TR: 8.6 Listen and point. **2** TR: 8.7 Listen and say. **3** Play and say.

SONG AND VALUE: *Take care of animals.*

LESSON 4

1 TR: 8.8 Listen and point. **2** TR: 8.9 Listen and sing. **3** TR: 8.10 Sing and do. **4** Stick.

VALUE

Take care of animals.

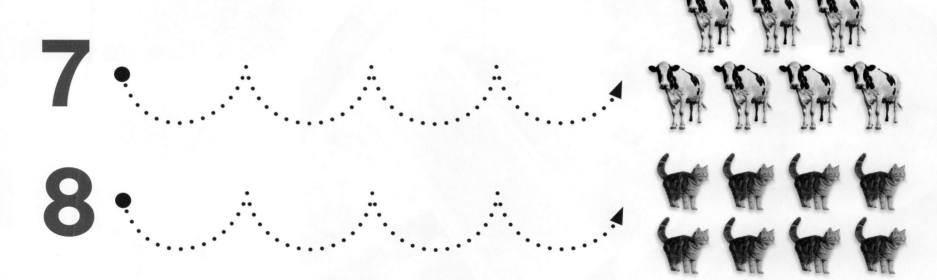

7

8

LESSON
5

NUMBERS: 7, 8

1 TR: 8.11 Listen and point. **2** TR: 8.12 Listen. Trace and say. **3** TR: 8.13 Listen and chant. **4** Draw and count.

51

 VIDEO Content Words: *egg, wool*

LESSON 6

1 Look and see.   **2** SC: 16 Watch.   **3** SC: 16 Watch, point, and say.

LESSON 7 PROJECT

1 Make.

My Clothes

Children with hats, Peru

NEW WORD: *hat*

1 Look and see.   **2** SC: 17 Watch.   **3** TR: 9.1 Listen and say.   **4** TR: 9.2 Listen and do.

LESSON 1

53

T-shirt

socks

shorts

shoes

jacket

black white brown

Girls at an ice festival, South Korea

LESSON
2

NEW WORDS: *jacket, shoes, shorts, socks, T-shirt; black, brown, white*
1 TR: 9.3 **Listen and point.**   **2** TR: 9.4 **Listen and say.**   **3** TR: 9.5 **Listen and chant.**

My T-shirt is orange.

My shorts are red.

STRUCTURE: *My T-shirt is orange. My shorts are red.*

1 TR: 9.6 **Listen and point.** **2** TR: 9.7 **Listen and say.** **3 Play and say.**

55

SONG AND VALUE: *Dress yourself.*

1 TR: 9.8 **Listen and point.**   **2** TR: 9.9 **Listen and sing.**   **3** TR: 9.10 **Sing and do.**   **4 Stick.**

VALUE

Dress yourself.

U u

umbrellabird

U
Uu

u

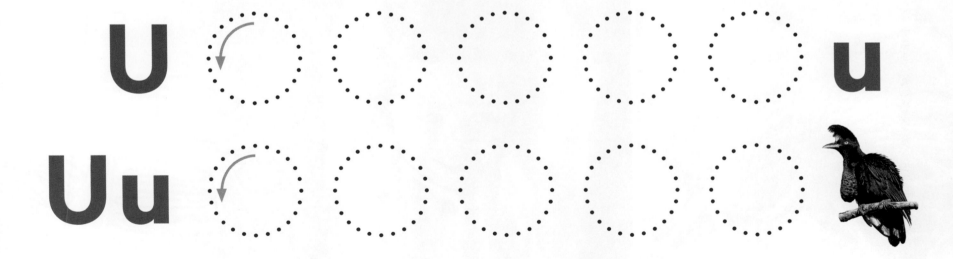

LETTERS AND SOUNDS: Uu, /ʌ/

1 TR: 9.11 Listen and point. **2** TR: 9.12 Listen. Trace and say. **3** TR: 9.13 Listen and chant. **4** Draw and say.

57

LESSON **6**

VIDEO **Content Words:** *scarf, sweater, yarn*

1 Look and see. **2** SC: 18 Watch. **3** SC: 18 Watch, point, and say.

LESSON **7**

PROJECT

1 Make.

Outside

Dumpy tree frogs in the
rain, Indonesia

LESSON 1

NEW WORD: *frog*

1 Look and see. **2** SC: 19 Watch. **3** TR: 10.1 Listen and say. **4** TR: 10.2 Listen and do.

rainbow

The Alps, Italy

flower

tree

bird

leaf

fish

NEW WORDS: *bird, fish, flower, leaf, rainbow, tree*

1 TR: 10.3 Listen and point.   **2** TR: 10.4 Listen and say.   **3** TR: 10.5 Listen and chant.

How many birds?

Four birds.

STRUCTURE: *How many birds? Four birds.*

1 TR: 10.6 **Listen and point.**   **2** TR: 10.7 **Listen and say.**   **3 Play and say.**

61

Three parrots, Costa Rica

VALUE

Explore outside.

SONG AND VALUE: *Explore outside.*

1 TR: 10.8 Listen and point.   **2** TR: 10.9 Listen and sing.   **3** TR: 10.10 Sing and do.   **4** Stick.

LESSON 5

NUMBERS: 9, 10

1 TR: 10.11 Listen and point.   **2** TR: 10.12 Listen. Trace and say.   **3** TR: 10.13 Listen and chant.   **4** Draw and count.

63

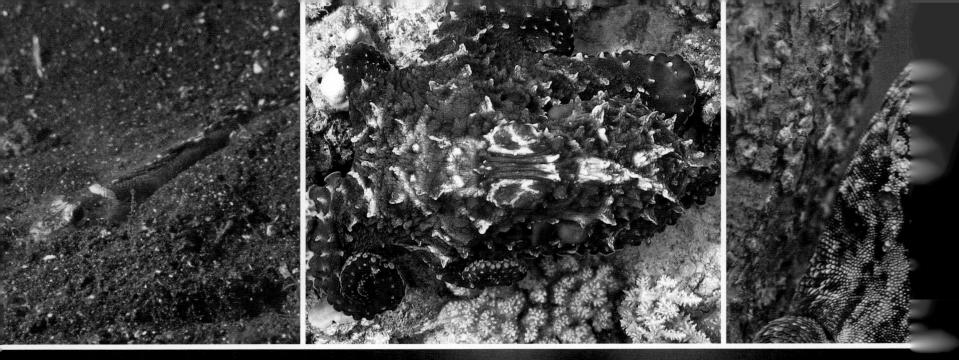

VIDEO   Content Words: *bug, lizard*

1 Look and see.   **2** SC: 20 Watch.   **3** SC: 20 Watch, point, and say.

PROJECT

1 Make.

UNIT
1

Hello!

Hello, my friend.
How are you?
I'm fine, thank you.
I'm fine, too.

[Chorus]
Let's say hello!
Let's make friends.
Let's make friends together.

Hello, my friend.
How are you?
I'm fine, thank you.
I'm fine, too.

[Chorus]

UNIT
2

School

What's this?
It's a book.
It's my book.
My nice, new book!

Take care of your book.
Take care of your things.

What's this?
It's a pencil.
It's my pencil.
My nice, new pencil!

Take care of your pencil.
Take care of your things.

UNIT
4

Toys

I have a car.
And I have a car.
Two cars—one and two.
One for me and one for you.

Let's share the cars.
Let's share the toys!

I have a ball.
And I have a ball.
Two balls—one and two.
One for me and one for you.

Let's share the balls.
Let's share the toys!

UNIT
3

Colors

Here is red and yellow, too.
Here is green and blue.

[Chorus]
Look at the colors,
beautiful colors!
What colors can you see?

Here is green and yellow, too.
Here is red and blue.

[Chorus]

UNIT 5

Let's Move!

Move your arms.
Move your hands.
Up and down,
arms and hands.

[Chorus]
Let's be active:
one, two, three!
Move your body.
Move with me!

Touch your legs.
Touch your feet.
Hands down,
and touch your feet.

[Chorus]

UNIT 6

Food

I like apples.
I like oranges.
I like bananas, too.

[Chorus]
Look at the food.
It's healthy food.
Food for me and you.

I like bananas.
I like apples.
I like oranges, too.

[Chorus]

On the Farm

What's this? Is it a horse?
Yes, it is. It's a horse.
It's my horse, Maxi.
Here you are, Maxi.
This is for you.

Take care of your horse.
Take care of animals.

What's this? Is it a goat?
No, it isn't. It's a lamb.
It's my lamb, Suzy.
Here you are, Suzy.
This is for you.

Take care of your lamb.
Take care of animals.

UNIT
7

My Family

Hello, Grandma. This is for you.
This is for me?
Oh, thank you! Thank you!
A nice surprise for me.

[Chorus]
Be good to your family.
All your family.

Hello, Grandpa. This is for you.
A hug for me?
Oh, thank you! Thank you!
A nice, big hug for me.

[Chorus]

68

UNIT
9

My Clothes

I have a jacket.
Look at my jacket.
My jacket is yellow.

Put on your jacket,
your yellow jacket.
Dress yourself today.

I have two shoes.
Look at my shoes.
My shoes are white.

Put on your shoes,
your white shoes.
Dress yourself today.

UNIT
10

Outside

[Chorus]
Come outside.
Explore outside.
Explore outside with me!

Look at the birds.
How many birds?
Three birds—one, two, three.

[Chorus]

Look at the flowers.
How many flowers?
Three flowers—one, two, three.

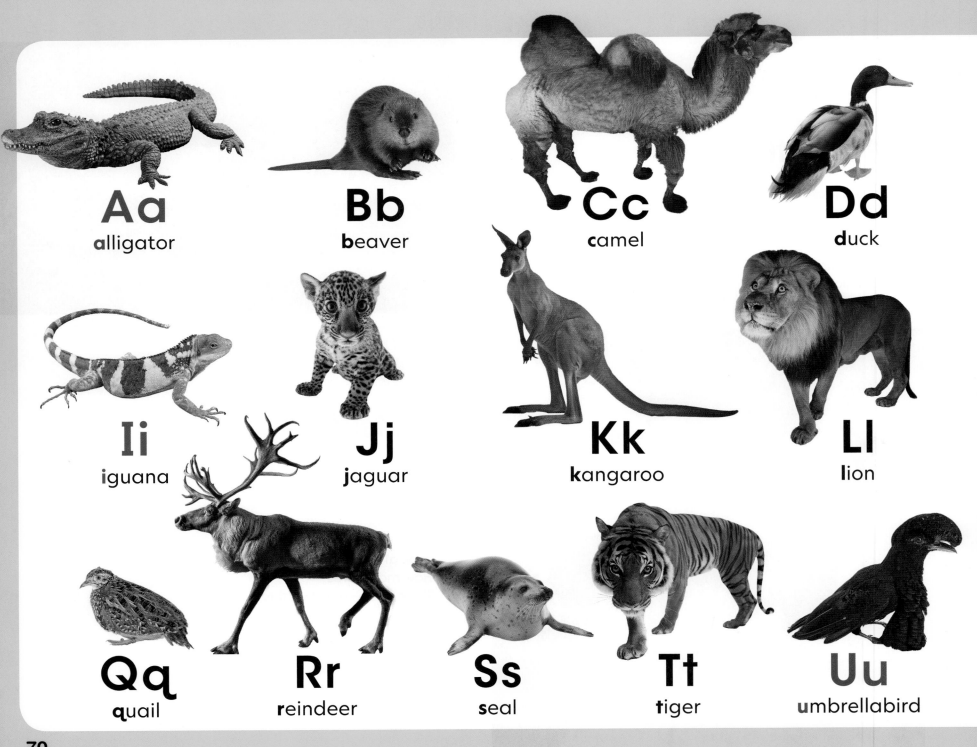

Aa
alligator

Bb
beaver

Cc
camel

Dd
duck

Ii
iguana

Jj
jaguar

Kk
kangaroo

Ll
lion

Qq
quail

Rr
reindeer

Ss
seal

Tt
tiger

Uu
umbrellabird

Ee
elephant

Ff
fish

Gg
gorilla

Hh
hippo

Mm
monkey

Nn
numbat

Oo
octopus

Pp
panda

Vv
vulture

Ww
wolf

Xx
fox

Yy
yak

Zz
zebra

CREDITS